A Parade of Poems.

Poems by Amy Danforth ✓
Illustrations by Carol McLeod

CRICKET PUBLICATIONS

Sylvania, Ohio

A Parade of Poems

ISBN 0-912883-03-0

For my Grandmother, Irene McCreery—A.D.
In memory of Janet Kishpaugh—C.M.

VALENTINE'S DAY

My valentines are all passed out
And I can hardly wait to see
The valentines inside my box
That all my friends have given me.

MY KITE

I love to fly my little kite.

Why does it always seem to be,

As soon as it is in the air,

It heads right for the nearest tree?!

IF I WERE A DUCK

To be a duck and not a boy!

Each time it rained, I'd quack for joy.

I'd find a puddle, splash and quack,

And watch the rain roll off my back!

SPRING FLOWERS

I've flowers on my windowsill:

Some tulips and a daffodil.

They brighten up a cloudy day

And bring inside the month of May.

BUILDING A NEST

A piece of string, a broken twig
Are things birds like the best.
In spring they go to look for them
And start to build their nest.

SPRING GRASS

The grass is getting green and tall—
The rains have helped to make it sprout.
I know for sure that it is spring
When people get their mowers out.

JUMPING ROPE

We need two people at the ends
To twirl the rope around,
Another standing in between
To jump above the ground.

WEEDING

Last week my garden was so clean—
There was not one weed to be seen
But now they've all grown back and so,
It's time again to get my hoe.

THE KOOL-AID STAND

I have a nickle in my hand.

I'll spend it at the Kool-Aid stand.

And when my first cup is all done—

Why, then I'll have another one.

LAZY SUMMER DAYS

In summer I like to be lazy—
Just lie in my hammock and swing.
Some people will think that I'm crazy
To lie there and not do a thing.

SHELLING

When the tide is very low,
Up and down the beach I go.
For the sea has left behind
Many things for me to find.

BEGINNING OF SCHOOL

My Mother says to go to school,

I need some scissors, crayons, glue.

I'll go and buy these things today,

Some pencils and a school box, too!

GLUE

On Monday morn I used my glue.

I thought I put the cap on tight.

Today I have no glue to use—

It all leaked in my desk last night.

ROLLER SKATING

Now I have four wheels
Strapped upon my feet.
How I love to put them on
And go rolling down the street.

INDIAN TEEPEES

Indian teepees made of hides,

With symbols painted on all sides.

A teepee is just like a tent

The Indians took where they went.

PUMPKINS

Last June I planted pumpkin seeds.

I watered them and pulled the weeds.

It's fall and Halloween is near;

The pumpkin-picking time is here!

JACK-O-LANTERN

Here's an eye, there's a nose.

This is where the mouth goes.

Add some ears, eyebrows, too.

He is ready now are you?

THE CHIPMUNK

We have a little chipmunk,
Who lives beneath our wall.
He always has his cheeks full.
How does he hold it all?

FALL FROLIC

This is the time of year we rakc
The leaves in a gigantic heap.
And when it's high, we'll scatter it
With every jump and every leap.

WINTER

My gloves are on,
My scarf is tied.
I'm ready now
To go outside.

WINTERTIME FUN

Sing a song of winter—
Sleds and skates and snow,
Frosty breath and snowmen.
How I love it so!

A TRAIN

A train is always fun to ride.

It often sways from side to side.

And every time we round a bend,

I see the last car at the end.

WINTER EVENINGS

Darkness now falls quicker,

While inside fires flicker.

Winter's come at last

With its icy blast.

Amy Danforth lives in Sylvania, Ohio with her husband and two young children. She has a wide variety of interests and never enough time to do them all. Amy gets many of the ideas for her stories from her children, as well as from her own childhood memories.

Carol McLeod is a professional musician and songwriter. She teaches music at Sand Creek Elementary School in Sand Creek, Michigan. Art has always been a hobby for her and she has done several portraits for friends and relatives. Her favorite subjects are children. This book is her first attempt at illustrating for children, but she says it felt very natural because "at school, I draw with the students a lot. We love to illustrate the songs we sing."

JE

Danforth, Amy.

Parade of poems